Fi

Essential Travel Tips – all you NEED to know

Table of Contents

Chapter 1: Introduction

Picture Courtesy: Liveaboard.com

Fiji, officially known as the Republic of Fiji is basically an island country consisting of 332 islands and thousands of islets. The majority of these islands were formed because of a volcanic eruption, almost 150 million years ago. It was a country that practiced cannibalism and was out of touch with civilization, but today it has become a contributor to the world economy, albeit a nominal one. Fiji is now a much progressive country with a vast promising future. It is estimated that by the year 2020, it will be enjoying a 2.2 billion dollartourism industry alone. This development has been possible due to its natural diversity and geographical advantage. There are numerous forests with great mineral resources that have made Fiji attract tourists. In this country one can surely be ensconced deep into Mother

Nature's lap and can enjoy heaven on earth. Today Fiji gains its chief income from its tourism industry that is growing heavily.

Fijian culture is rich witha core tradition. They believe in their past and maintain that even now with the same customs and traditions. In fact Fijian culture can be considered as the amalgamation of various cultures such as the Indo-Fijian, Asian and a little bit of European. From language to food, they have their special and unique variations as the essence of their culture. They have the most vibrant culture and attitude and favor a simple and down to earth nature which makes it more interesting for the tourists. Fiji as a country is very unique and shows that without getting influenced by any other culture. Fiji's past has witnessed various cultures beingintroduced to its tradition and now in the present day, there are various cultures in Fiji that have come together to create something of a multicultural identity.

Chapter 2: Things You Must Know About Fiji

Picture Courtesy: TropicalIslands64

The mesmerizing beauty of the landscapes and the beautiful sea, nature in its best form, the super catchy tradition of this amazing country makes Fiji a land of adventure and mystery. Unveil the great mysteries from the corners of this land. This country offers everything that you lack in the busy metro life.

1. The Land of Many Lands

Fiji is basically a land of 332 islands. Apart from the islands, Fiji has a large number of islets. Due to a volcanic eruption about 150 million years ago, the islands of Fiji came into existence. Several of these islands hold a large part of the populace and among them Viti Levu has the largest population. Though some of the islands are not habitable due to the terrain, they are quite accessible. .

2. Three Official Languages

Fiji is among the few nations with three official languages. According to the nationalconstitution Fiji has English, Fijian and Fiji Hindi as the official languages. In fact there are 200 different dialects. Fijian has the most varieties of dialects and they are spoken more than the other official languages.

3. They Play Rugby

Rugby is considered the most important sport in Fiji and the national sport as well. Their national team is one of the most successful rugby teams in the world. They are famous for their seven-a-side form of the game. Rugby has a very significant place in the hearts of every Fijian. They are all very proud of this sport and their team.

4. Cannibalism, a Part of their History

It is one of the most interesting facts about Fiji is that once cannibalism was very much a part of their life until Christianity came into this country. According to the archaeologists this practice was about 2500 years old. There are various evidences to prove this fact. There were many speculations about this practice and many questions are yet to be answered. There were many beliefs behind it.

5. Their Traditional Dishes

The traditional dishes of Fiji are very famous. They are unique in their way mostly because all the Fijian cuisines come directly from their tradition without having any influence of other cultures. They have their own distinctive flavors. They have a very unique way to cook. The traditional method is known as Lovo. These lovo pits are the secret to creating such amazing dishes.

6. Traditional Drink is Kava

Kava can be considered as the national drink of Fiji and not only the traditional one. Kava is basically the ground root of a plant that is from a pepper family. Kava is not only enjoyed as a drink but the Fijians believe it has many medicinal qualities that help heal insomnia, stress and other depression related issues. Kava is often called Yaqona in different regions. It is one of the must have drinks for the Fijians for all their ceremonies and festivals.

7. The Booming Industry of Tourism

This is one of the most interesting points about Fiji. Though this might come as a surprise, Fiji is considered as one of the major contributor to the world of tourism. Yes this 'land of many lands' shows some promising scopes for the future. Fiji's tourism industry is growing every year. It is estimated that at the end of 2020 Fiji will be earning an amount of 2.2 billion or may be more from tourism. This aspect of Fiji is surely amazing considering their overall population which is less than 1 million.

8. *The Practice of Walking on Hot Stone*

The fire walking ceremony is actually one of the most famousactivities in Fiji.It was the Sawau tribe that started this tradition. And they have been at it since generations. This tradition is still going strong. And you can see them walking on hot stones that are still on fire.

9. *They have the Finest Water*

Fiji has the finest water. In fact a prominent branded water company has the same source of water as the Fijians have. The clear crystal and pure water is one of the most amazing things of Fiji.

10. *You can Jump From Yesterday to Today in Fiji*

This is really interesting. In Fiji you can actually jump from today to yesterday or vice versa. Fiji is located on the International Date Line which is an imaginary line which has a spot where if you stand exactly on the line your half body will be in today andthe other half in yesterday. It is like on one side of the line the day ends and the other half the day starts.

Summarizing: Fiji is very much attached to its roots and culture and its unique traditions. Fijians are modern and contribute a significant amount to the world of tourism. Still they are living with their very own roots and traditions without getting distracted by the outer world. This is the basic quality of Fiji that attracts thousands of tourists every years to witness this amazing land.

Chapter 3: Best Places to Visit in Fiji

Picture Courtesy:<u>Fiji - Rough Guides</u>

A paradise in the South Pacific Ocean, Fiji often comes at the top part of the bucket list of people who love to travel and explore new places. Made up of more than 300 islands, Fiji is the perfect getaway with your family and friends and the number of tourist spots and adventure destinations present there will surely not disappoint you. The beaches, the large expanse of turquoise sea, the coconut trees, the rainforests, the exotic flora and fauna, the coral reefs, you name it and everything is there. A number of beautiful and stunning resorts and fun-filled activities will make Fiji a holiday to remember for a long time. Suva, the capital of Fiji and Nadi are the two main places and have the international airports, and access to the other islands becomes convenient from here. So embark on this magical journey and enjoy Fiji to the fullest.

1. *Mamanuca and Yasawa Islands*

It is true that there are a large number of islands to choose from in Fiji but if you are looking for a picture perfect spot that can take your breath away, Mamanuca and Yasawa Islands should definitely be your top spots. Mamanuca is also the closest island present near the international airport of Fiji in a place called Nadi and thus is the first convenient tourist spot. The large expanse of sandy white beaches, the never-ending sea glittering in turquoise and the slight swaying of the coconut trees to gentle breeze makes the area perfect for relaxing. The best way to experience these islands would be through the Blue Lagoon Cruise which takes you on a cruise around these group of islands and also lets you spend ample amount of time there.

2. *Bouma National Heritage Park, Taveuni Island*

Fiji is not only about beaches and the sea. It has a lush green covering of rainforests extending extensively. To feel the natural beauty of Fiji to the maximum you should visit this national park in Taveuni Island. Set up as early as the 1990s, this 150 square kilometres area is the perfect spot for hikers, adventurers, nature lovers and wildlife enthusiasts as it houses some of the rarest tropical plants and a large number of diverse birds. Provisions for snorkeling in Waitabu, hiking to Vidawa and taking a plunge at the Tavoro waterfalls are also made. The park also houses Lake Tagimaucia, famous for the Tagimoucia flowers.

3. Beqa Lagoon, Viti Levu

This tourist spot is a favorite for divers from all around the world and the main attraction is the Beqa Lagoon Shark Dive, where they come face-to-face with one of the most feared creatures, the bull shark, the blacktip reef shark, the whitetip reef shark and if luck permits, the tiger shark. There are more than 100 diving sites present and you can choose one according to the experience you want. This is the best place to be if you can't accommodate deep sea diving in your schedule. The Beqa Island is where the Sawau tribe lives and you can even enjoy their local traditions and ceremonies.

4. Sri Siva Subramaniya Temple, Nadi

The largest and the most famous, drawing tourists from world across, the Hindu temple of the Southern Hemisphere is not present in India but in the island of Nadi in Fiji. The majestic Dravidian architecture can be witnessed in this temple and the colorful paintings and frescoes on the ceilings, painted by artists from India, have awed not only the devotees but also tourists of other faiths.

The temple is in the name of God Mungan, a major Hindu God of South India. Be sure to follow the stringent rules once you enter the temple premises.

5. Great Astrolabe Reef, Kadavu

Kadavu is the fourth largest island of Fiji and it has a vast expanse of around 100 kilometres of the Great Barrier Reef, making it the fourth largest in the world. Deep sea diving has changed the perspective of the life of many individuals and if you want to have the same experience, this is the place to be. Delve into the underwater experience of tunnels, drop-offs, caverns, amyriad of corals and be surrounded by tropical fishes. If you want to snorkel, you can do that as well, from shallow locations and swim with the famous manta rays. The reef also has a number of billfish species like tuna and trevally and you can even fish in designated areas.

6. Garden of Sleeping Giants, Viti Levu

Located in the foothills of glorious mountain peaks of Viti Levu is the Garden of Sleeping Giants, which is the main attraction for people who love plants. Housing a large variety of species of Orchids and water pond lilies along with frogs and tadpoles, it gives a very serene and peaceful aura to the place. Littered with swings and hammocks, you can spend a major portion of the day here. Once you are done, you can head to the Sabeto Hot Springs and Mud Pool and take a therapeutic bath there.

7. *Navua River*

This 65 kilometer long river flows from Viti Levu to the South Coast and is lined by magnificent greenery, rainforests, canyons and waterfalls, making it a special boat ride. You can paddle on canoes or kayaks, use a bamboo raft called bilibili and even challenge the rapids in an inflatable raft. You can even explore the villages that fall on the way and participate in their ceremonies and get to know the real Fiji, not the fancy one.

8. *Sawa-i-Lau caves, Yasawa Islands*

The most famous aspect of these caves are the limestone caverns shaped by waves and wind. The pools are easy to access and you can swim there in the crystal clear water and relax. You can even go to the inner caves through an underwater tunnel which is only accessible during low tides.

9. *Kula Eco Park, Viti Levu*

This eco-park is located in Sigatoka and is the house to a number of endangered species like Fijian Crested Iguana. There are wooden boardwalks present to take you through the forests and you can enjoy the beauty of tropical plants, snakes, lizards, birds, tropical fishes etc.

10. Levuka, Ovalau

It is a UNESCO Heritage site and was also the place where the first Europeans settled down in Fiji. The old buildings made of wood and the ambience of the town gives you an idea of Fiji during the 19th century and the mango and coconut trees surrounding it contribute to the quaint environment.

Summarizing: These are the main places to visit while you are in Fiji, though there are many other sites which may not be a major tourist attraction but are as beautiful. A local guide will know about these places, so make sure you hire one. The places mentioned above are the must-visit ones and do not miss out on them at any cost.

Chapter 4: Best Islands to Visit in Fiji

Picture Courtesy: YouTube

Fiji is a small country consisting almost 332 islands and thousands of islets; altogether it makes a wonderful holiday destination that attracts thousands of tourists every year. The number is increasing every year with promising results in the future. The great climate and the spectacular geographical setting of the islands makes Fiji one of the best.

1. Viti Levu

Viti Levu is the largest island in Fiji. It is considered as the international gateway of Fiji. This island is the best place you can stay to enjoy your Fijian vacation. It has some of the most famous resorts and hotels in Fiji. Apart from its international status and recognition, Viti Levu has an interesting side to it. Away from the tourist spots, there are many small villages you can go and travel to. The mountain ranges, the beautiful tropical jungles, the waterfalls, all of them will mesmerize you with their beauty. The Garden of the Sleeping Giant in the beautiful foot hills is a place that you can go and explore. The Natadola beach is one of the prettiest beaches in Fiji.

2. Taveuni

If you are a nature lover and want to explore the deepest secrets hidden within nature then Taveuni is your place. It is a perfect place for hiking and experiencing the country's most authentic traditions. Also known as the Garden isle, this place is just like heaven on earth. The lush forests, the beautiful cool waterfalls are what you need to see here. Here the Bouma National Heritage Park is famous for preserving the rare tropical bloom and the bird watching. This island is packed with natural goodness and is the best spot to relax and meditate surrendering yourself to Mother Nature.

3. The Mamanuca Island

The magnificent Mamanuca Island is one of the most famous holiday islands in Fiji. Here you will find the best weather in Fiji with plenty of sunshine. The cool blue water and those white sands make it one of the most beautiful beaches. It is the perfect example of what is called the quintessential tropical beauty. In fact the famous Tom Hanks movie Cast Away was filmed here on this island. On this island you will find many luxurious resorts to stay as well. When in Fiji this island should stay on your priority list.

4. *Vanua Levu*

This is the second largest island in Fiji, though it is not as crowded as Viti Levu, but this island surely attracts most of the tourists to spend their holiday. Here the Wasali Nature Reserve and the water falls are the famous ones that tourists must visit. Look out for the panoramic views and capture your moment for the best Instagram feed. This is a perfect place for the best pictures. This shelter bay is a popular place for the sailors. Apart from its great scenic beauty other activities that you can indulge in here are hiking, mountain biking and many other things.

5. *Kadavu*

This is the most unspoilt group of Islands that you will find in Fiji. These islands are a tourist pleaser and they provide some of the best scenic beauties of the sea and the natural surroundings. The interiors of this place are decorated with a virgin rainforest and vast volcanic peaks. Here you will find an impressive diversity of birds like Velvet dve, Kavadu Musk parrot and the Crimson Shining parrot. There are not many resorts here that you can stay in. But there are some eco-resorts along the coast with pretty sights of the beach and beautiful gardens.

6. *Yasawa Islands*

Located in a very remote place this island may be under developed but equally stunning as the rest of the islands. You might have seen this beautiful island on the backgound of the famous film 'The Blue Lagoon'. This island is another great example of tropical beauty. The crystal clear water and serene nature will fill your senses to the core. Here you can indulge in various activities, like swimming, hiking or even kayaking. Explore this beautiful island. This may not be a popular place to stay but definitely worthy of staying, and once you experience this place you might not want to go to other places.

7. *Wakaya Island*

This island is famous for its luxurious resorts and spa therapies. This place is privately owned by many celebrities. The turquoise water, the silver color beautiful sands and the pleasant weather all make it an amazing pace to spend your holiday. Other features like water sports, kayaking, swimming and spending your time under the sun will be some of the best memories of your life. Take out your phone start shooting some pictures and selfies here on the Wakaya Island.

8. *Suva*

Suva is one of the best places to stay in Fiji. It is the centre place in Fiji and one of the most famous tourist destinations. It is said that Suva is the natural treasure of Fiji and the best thing you can do in Fiji is to explore Suva from sunrise to sunset. It has the beautiful blue waters and the perfect white sand. You can just spend your entire day here under the sun. The weather of Suva is amazing. Lie down under the sun and have that perfect sun tan and forget all your worries here in Suva. Some of the greatest luxurious resorts, restaurants and clubs of Fiji are located in Suva.

9. *Vatulele*

Located in the south of Viti Velu, this idyllic island is covered with palms and rainforests. Here you will find four beautiful villages on this island. This island is known as the major producer of tapa clothing. Famous for its archaeological sites, Vatulele has some of the oldest ancient rock paintings in the limestone caves and the pools. Activities like the swimming, kayaking and hiking are some of the great things you can do in these villages. Whatever fun things you have do, do not forget to atleast visit the villages. Through the villages you wlll be able to come close to the true Fijian culture and traditions.

10. *Matangi Private Island*

This is the perfect island to spend the time for new couples. This private island has some of the most luxurious resorts. This is one of the best places for a destination wedding and many couples choose them as their honeymoon spot too. The beautiful coral reefs and the seductive white sand beach is something that will attract you all the time. This Island has the best view of sunset. This island is a great example of paradise and spending your holiday will be like being in one.

Summarizing: The land of lands has some of the beat islands in the world. Tourists from different parts of the world come here to witness these beautiful islands that have so many things to offer.

Chapter 5: Best Beaches in Fiji

Picture Courtesy:<u>TravelOnline</u>

The beautiful blue water and the white sand spread over for kilometers, the beautiful geographical settings of the mountains and the lush green rainforests, all of these are just perfect for your trip. In Fiji it is the treasure you will hold in your memories for the rest of your life.

1. Honeymoon Beach

This is one of the best beaches in Fiji. This picture perfect beach is famous for its white sand which is framed with rocky headlands and lined with beautiful, leaning palm trees. This beach is not much crowded and has only limited accommodation option. But being a private Fijian island it is only available if your book it in advance, that way you might get it for your holiday. This is famous among couples so it will be one of the best memories for your life, here on the Honeymoon Beach.

2. Liku Beach

Located in the Mamanuca Island this beach has something special about it. This west-facing beach is best for spending your day under the sun. The breezy wind and the beautiful sound of the sea will give you the ultimate peace that you have been looking for in your life. The blue water and the calm ambience will make you feel as if you are somewhere else in this busy world.

3. Natadola Beach

This beach can just be called a piece of heaven on earth. Just 30 minutes away from Nadi, this beach is one of the most famous beaches in Fiji. Rich with beautiful coral reefs, Natadola beach is best known for its swim-worthy water. If you are interested in snorkeling then head out to the end of the beach for an excellent round of snorkeling. .

4. Yasawa Island Beach

This beach is one of the best beaches in Fiji. This beach reaches up to the sky and plunges onto white sand shores. Covered in grassland this beach is perfect for strolling around and exploring the island. The white sand and the beautiful blue water will keep you calm and cool throughout the day. This beach has the first ever beachfront spa, where you can go and relax. The area has many luxurious bungalows on this beach where you can stay and enjoy Fiji at its best.

5. Namale Private Beach

This is the most luxurious beach in the whole of Fiji. The Namale Resort and Spa provides some of the best quality special treatment that will make you feel like royalty. There are at least three staffs to one guest, attending to them for their various needs. This private beach is best for a cocktail party with a beautiful private pool under the shade of the coconut trees. Many celebrities are regular visitors of this beach. Other temptations such as scuba diving, hiking to a secret water fall etc. will attract you the most.

6. Seagrass Bay

The crystal clear water of this place is the main attraction of this beach. It is also one of the best places for snorkeling. If you want to stay here and spend your holiday on this amazing island beach than you certainly can as there are almost 25 beautiful villas waiting for you with their luxurious treatments. This is one of the most dazzling beaches that you cannot miss.

7. Vomo Island

This island features some of the best beaches in Fiji and the best spots for snorkeling. The western beach is the best one that you can enjoy. This island may look a bit deserted but is best once you have experienced it. There is the famous Vomo Island Resort where you can go and enjoy your holiday.

8. Malolo Island

Malolo Island is said to have the softest and deepest sand in the world. This island will give you the access to some of the most beautiful beaches and aqua marine waters. This place has the most famous bars where you can have some of the delicious cocktails of coconut flavors. You can indulge in snorkeling or scuba diving or just relax on a hammock and read a good book. Here nothing will worry you.

9. Castaway Island

This amazing island is encircled by beautiful white sand beaches and gorgeous coral reefs. It got its name from its sole and famous resort the Castaway Resort. This beach will offer you some of the best views of Fiji. You can just stroll around the beach taking pictures or just enjoy the great weather and the blue sea. Here you can also avail a service of a helicopter that will take you to the mainland. The facilities of this resort are top class and you will remember your days here forever.

10. Qamea Island

The beach of Qamea is known as the most magnificent beach in Fiji. Here you will be able to see the beautiful tropical rainforest and the volcanic peaks if you are in the mood for exploring. Otherwise you can just relax on the beach with a nice cocktail along your side and you can enjoy a perfect sunbath. Here you can stay in the lavish resort of Qamea.

Summarizing: For Fiji It is the beaches that are the most tempting attraction for all the tourists. Fiji has some of the most famous beaches in the world. Also the great resorts that are perfect for your stay.

Chapter 6: Souvenirs You Must Buy inFiji

Picture Courtesy: Travel Associates

Souvenirs are one of the greatest things you can buy from a trip. It adds that extra charm to your memories. Apart from the pictures these souvenirs are the best way to sieve through the memories.

1. *Mako Masks*

These masks are basically made of wood with turtle carvings or paintings on them. These masks used to represent the different gods and deities as well as many other ideas like happiness, strength and prosperity. All of these have a special significance in the Fijian culture. These masks are one of the special features of Fiji and definitely one of the best souvenirs you can buy from here. These masks can be colorful and can be of different shapes. Each of them have a different meaning, so while buying them you can ask the shopkeeper about the meaning of the mask and buy accordingly.

2. Bula Shirt

A Bula shirt is a must have while vacationing in Fiji. We all know the famous shirts of Hawaii and how much it means to have one. Well in case of Fiji it is quite the same. The Bula shirt is another one among the best souvenirs you can buy from Fiji. You can get it in different colors and sizes. They are normally short sleeved with attached buttons with flower patterns on them. They are all very comfortable and made out of cotton. So while vacationing or roaming around the beach try to buy one and have a great picture for your Instagram feed.

3. Fiji Pearls

Fiji pearls are said to be the rarest pearls for their unique colors. As we know pearls are white or sometimes colored with pink or sky blue highlights. But the pearls of Fiji are chocolate brown in color and they look so different than the normal pearls but are very attractive and alluring. In Fiji there are various pearl farms where a lot research is conducted on the pearls. You can get a tour of that place as well. Here you will get the opportunity to buy the pearls from the farm directly. Prices may vary, it can start from 50$ to 1000$ for a single pearl.

4. Forks and Figures

Fiji's past with cannibalism is known to everyone. In fact you can find many mementos for that history still available in the markets, though these mementos are basically for buying as souvenirs from Fiji. These handcrafted cannibal forks comes in all sorts of sizes and shapes. They look very unique and so different that you will definitely buy them. You go for a street-side shop or some other shops where you will be able to find the wooden forks. Also you can look for cannibal figures which are made from coconut shells. Those are kind of creepy but worth buying.

5. Pottery

Fiji's pottery can be very unique and distinctive. Their hand-made pottery is well known among the locals and the tourists. While in Fiji one of these pieces are a must-have. Nakabuta and Lawai are the two places where you can get the best pottery. They are famous for making their traditional pottery. All of these are crafted by hand and then fired in an open fire. You can even watch them while they are being made. It is so delightful and artistically inspiring to see these get made. Other than this village, you can get these in super markets or street-side markets. Not only pots you can get various things from here like jewelry, animal figures, bowls etc. These sets of pottery can be very good gifts for your friends and family.

6. Spa Products

The natural essence and pure ingredients make all the products of Fiji very organic and best for your skin. When in

Fiji you will understand the greatness of these natural products which are pure bliss. From hair to skin products you will get various types of beauty creams and lotions. In fact the local skin care products and spa products are the best. You can get an appointment for a wonderful spa experience from any spa around here. Or you can buy these products for your home and family as well.

7. *Lali Drum*

This is another special feature of Fijian culture. It is used as a form of communication in Fiji. These drums have a great significance. In the past it was through these drums many important announcements were done in various events. These are made of wood and hollowed logs. These drums are different than the normal drums as the sticks are made of wood too. These drums can be a bit big for you to take them home. But if you search properly, you might get a smaller one and something more decorative than the normal ones. These drums are one of the best souvenirs from Fiji.

8. *Kava Products*

Any occasion or ceremony is incomplete without serving kava in it. This Fijian drink is one of the must-have staple drinks for everyone. This drink is made of ground yaqona root. The processing of this drink is very easy. They powder is first strained through a cloth and mixed with water. Then that is mixed with a muddy looking substance before serving as a drink. This kava drink can have a slight tingling or numbing effect but this is absolutely fine. And there's nothing illegal about it. You can purchase this kava powder anywhere in the supermakets or other shops. There are no restrictions on bringing a pack of kava powder in your bag.

9. Tapa Painting

Tapa painting can be a great souvenir for your friends and families. These paintings are basically different shapes of paintings in different patterns. There is an abstract feeling in these paintings. It can be used as a great wall hanging or tapestry. These paintings are made on clothes and on paper made of the bark of the mulberry trees. The dyes that are used in the products are made from natural products and terracotta clay.

10. Turtle Carvings

Turtle carvings have a significant place in the Fijian culture for being the a token of good luck. Turtles are widely associated with this culture. Once Fiji was a country that used to consume turtle on a large scale, but later the Fiji Fisheries Act prohibited the killing of sea turtles. The turtle carvings are widely famous in Fiji and you will be able to find out this souvenir as bowls, pots and may other items.

Summarizing: Every souvenir of Fiji carries a great significance of their culture. From very ordinary to a unique product you will get everything from this traditional island. The prices can vary according to the shapes and sizes. But if pursue correctly you will be able to buy all of these souvenirs for your home.

Chapter 7: Most Popular Night Destinations in Fiji

Picture Courtesy: <u>Tourism Fiji</u>

Fiji is often associated with a relaxed natural atmosphere far from every hustle and bustle, beside the calming sound of the sea. But after the sun is set and you have witnessed the beautiful orange hue on the sky, the darkness of Fiji brings out a different face of the country. There might not be the famous clubs of Ibiza or Dubai, but they surely will mesmerize you with their beauty with a hint of crazy clubbing nights.

1. Nightlife in Suva

Suva is one of the best night destinations in Fiji. It has some of the best clubs and bars that you will find in Fiji. From a great bar where you can groove all night long to a very sophisticated ideal romantic bar, you will find every kind of bar here. The cocktails and their special way of serving them will make you want more. There are some beach side clubs as well that you can visit for a night time party on the beach.

Down Under Pub Fiji: located on Suva Island, this pub cum bar will provide you with an awesome experience and a great idea of fabulous cocktails. This is one of the friendliest bars with the staff being cool and the service being A-class. Things like the pool tables and a fantastic atmosphere attract the tourists to this amazing pub.

2. Nightlife in Nadi

Nadi is another famous destination for night touring. If you love to spend your night with excitement and fun, then the pubs and the clubs of Nadi will make your wish come true. This island has some of the most unique kind of Pubs with various themes and attractions from famous DJ nights to Clubs going on until 4 am the next day; all the crazy stuff you will find in Nadi.

Ed's Bar: In Nadi the popular surf bar which is known as the Ed's Bar is one of the popular destinations for the locals as well as tourists. This bar has that great rustic feeling that you will love. If you are fond of beer then this bar is the ultimate place for you. With its outdoor beer garden this place is an ideal choice for you and your friends to come here and enjoy the happy hours that they provide.

3. Nightlife in Beachcomber

This island is mainly known as the party island for its perfect setting of bars and clubs all around the Mamanuca Island. Here you can stay an entire day swimming in the great waters, diving and surfing, then finally at night you will be able to see this island transforming into something that was not there during the day time. The actual action starts from that time. The night is filled with DJ nights and dancers. You will have the most fun in Beachcomber.

4. NightLife in Denarau Island

This island is one of the most famous islands in Fiji with lots of excitement. The perfect location of this island makes it more appealing to the tourists. There are various kinds of bars that you can visit here.

Nuku Restaurant & Bar: This bar is located just near the beach making it an amazing one for the tourists who love to be by the beach no matter what the time. After the sunset this place becomes so beautiful that the nightlife seems very different that the others. Nuku Restaurant and Bar is the great place from where you can have your drinks and at the same time enjoy the beautiful sunset and the serene beauty of the sea.

Summarizing: The nightlife during the week and weekends can be different, but most of the clubbing spots will give you the same vibe and excitement throughout the entire week. In fact you might be surprised to see the crowd they have every night. From sophisticated bars to crazy dance bars in Fiji, you will get the most of it, even the coolest bars near the beaches.

Chapter 8: Best Restaurants in Fiji

Picture Courtesy: <u>Musket Cove Island Resort</u>

The Fijian cuisine, there is something about it. And to savor it along with the authentic experience you need to hop into every restaurant that serves the best of Fijian cuisine. Some of these restaurants have the authentic atmosphere that will make you feel delightful and so close to the tradition.

1. *Nadina Fijian Restaurant*

To have the authentic Fijian experience you need to visit this restaurant at least once. This restaurant will give you the pure essence of Fiji through their delicious food and decor. While here try out the various traditonal Fijian dishes along with the famous kava. All of these dishes are made of fresh vegetables and fruits and are packed with goodness. In this restaurant try the Kokoda , this is one of the best dishes you can have here. This great dish with a unique taste of citrus and coconut cream will just make you want more.

2. The Eco Cafe

If you ask what is so great about Fiji apart from the traditional Fijian cuisine, well, then it will bE the charm of this amazing restaurant and the service of the staff. The Eco café is just like that, this place will serve you the best Fijian style pizza on the famous beach of the Coral Coast. The restaurant is situated right beside the beach and you can just enjoy your food while enjoying the beautiful surroundings of the sea and the beach. Apart from the pizza you will get a great menu of Italian food here in this restaurant.

3. Tokoriki Oishii Teppanyaki

Located in the Tokoriki Resort, this restaurant serves the best teppanyaki on the entire island. This restaurant is one of the best in Fiji and it seems to be a very busy restaurant. So if you want a table over here you must have an advanced booking otherwise a table here will be quite unaffordable. This popular restaurant is famous for is hibachi style cooking as well. Try out the wasabi beef here, it is the first choice of every customer here in this restaurant.

4. Tiko's Floating Restaurant

Yes exactly as the name suggest this restaurant is basically a floating restaurant as it is on a boat that is always at sea. Located in Suva this restaurant will give a different experience, along with the food experience the feel of eating on a floating restaurant right in the sea. This restaurant is famous for its seafood range with very reasonable prices. Try out the fish and steak here. You will get hooked in the wonderful environment that it offers.

5. Tu's Palace

This restaurant is famous for its traditional touch in almost everything on the menu. They use natural ingredients in a very authentic Fijian style. So you can just expect some of the greatest dishes here. Apart from the core Fijian dishes, it serves other cuisines as well, like Thai food, curry and grilled fish, to Asian Noodles. Here you can enjoy the food along with your family and it might become your instant favorite. It has a very homely atmosphere so it is great for kids too.

6. Governor's Museum Themed Restaurant

This restaurant is basically a restored colonial house where you will have the perfect dining experience. The décor will give you an historic feeling with those old photographs and newspaper clippings on the boards. This restaurant looks like a 19th century establishment with a hint of history. It will be a great experience to dine in this Governor's

Museum Themed restaurant. While in this restaurant try to order the Mahi Mahi, it is the best you can have here.

7. Bonefish Seafood Restaurant

Located on the Denarau Island this restaurant is famous for its seafood. They have the fresh cooked seafood that will be served on your table in a lovely setting on the patio waterfront. Try the crab curry here, it is one of the signature dishes in this restaurant.

8. The Rhum-ba

Enjoy the stunning views while experiencing the amazing food served by Rhum-ba. The menu of here specializes mainly in steak and seafood. This restaurant will give you the ultimate experience of dining. The sophisticated décor and the amazing style of preparation surely will win your heart. Enjoy your steak with a perfect cocktail on a beautiful evening.

9. Mathmacita Mexican Restaurant

In Fiji apart from great Fijian cuisine, you will get all kinds of cuisine from all over the world. The Mexican cuisine is one of the favourite cuisines here in Mamacita Mexican Restaurant. Get some great spices of Mexico here in Fiji with the tacos, taquitos and enchiladas. The menu has various ranges from fish to chicken to beef to fulfil your hunger. The selection of dishes is enough for you to get your mouth busy for the next half an hour. Enjoy your food along with the great live music.

10. *Sitar Indian and Thai Restaurant*

Indian food is the second most popular food in Fiji. And Sitar is the best restaurant that serves the best Indian food here in Fiji. Apart from Indian you will also get many Thai dishes as well. Sometimes they have a great mixed dishes of Indian and Thai curry that will make you want to order some more. This unique dish is very popular among the locals as well as the tourists. Located in Nadi , try the lamb curry of Sitar. It is one of the best here you will ever taste.

Summarizing: Food is the ultimate example of any tradition. And the Fijian cuisine is just like that. The authentic Fijian Cuisine is so tasty and healthy at e same time that you will not worry or watch out what you are eating. These were some of the best restaurants that you can go to, to have some of the best dishes served in Fiji along with the experience.

Chapter 9: Most Luxurious Resorts in Fiji

Picture Courtesy: <u>TravelPlusStyle.com</u>

The setting of the resorts right in the middle of nature will give you the opportunity to experience the tradition and the nature of the country you are vacationing in. So choosing a good resort is always a good idea. Some of the resorts of Fiji have top-class facilities with beautiful scenic beauties from where you can enjoy Fiji by yourself.

1. Shangri-La Resort and Spa

You will get the name of this resort in 'Lost Horizon' by British author James Hilton, written in 1933. Here this resort is described as an existence that is secluded from the rest of the world. And that is actually true. Located in the

Yanuca Island, this resort will offer you ultimate comfort and luxury in a very special way. Relax in the spa and receive the ultimate bliss for your body and soul.

2. Wakaya Club and Spa

This resort in Wakaya Island will spoil you with its lavish facilities and atmosphere. This private island is a favorite place for many celebrities. In this hotel you will find some of the best designed gardens and outdoor dining area where you can take a walk or just have a private moment. The interiors are very attractive with floor to ceiling windows. From here you will be able to watch the sea and the surroundings from inside your room. This resort is a perfect place to enjoy your holiday in Fiji.

3. Likuliku Lagoon Resort

This resort is in the shape of a crescent, located in the Malolo Island. According to Fijian mythology it is an important landmark in the history of Fiji. The design of this resort is very exclusive like the traditional Fijian village with the hand woven thatched roofs and famous tribal patterned interiors. This resort will give the authentic style of living like a Fijian.

4. Navutu Stars Resort

The spacious rooms, the high ceiling and the cram-hued walls are one of the best features of this beautiful resort. The resort doors are located in a way that once you open them, the alabaster beach front will open in front of you just like magic. This wonderful resort will offer you with some of the most beautiful panoramic views which you can just enjoy from your room. The Spa treatments and the yoga classes in the mornings are an absolute bliss. Watch the beautiful sunset and enjoy your stay in this lovely resort. .

5. Vomo Resort

This resort is a perfect exotic resort in Fiji. The interiors are sophisticated and the relaxed atmosphere will give you the best times here in Fiji. Get yourself the best treatment of Spa here in this resort along with the lovely food that it offers. You can also go out for swimming and hiking near the resort. There are lots of activities that you can do near the resort.

6. Royal Davui Island Resort

Located on a very private islet in the Beqa Lagoon this resort has 16 villas under it with the best service and top-class facilities. This resort is so much secluded from the outer world that you will feel like you are in a totally different part of the world. This resort is perfect for newly wedded couples as it will give them ultimate romantic atmosphere here. The romantic setting of this resort is appreciated by many. The relaxed and serene beauty of this islet will make your stay an amazing one.

7. Taveuni Island Resort and Spa

Taveuni is often mentioned as the Garden Island of Fiji. So a resort set on the top of this place will give you some of the great experiences of Fiji. From the resort you will be able to see the great Pacific ocean and its beauty. This resort is comprised of 12 lavish villas, it has a very beautiful spa as well where you can relax and the time will just pass. It is an ideal place if you want to explore nature.

8. Emaho Sekawa Resort

Not only the beautiful interiors from the inside, but this resort provides some of the best panoramic views of Fiji. This resort is simple beautiful along with its surroundings. You can see the horizon from here and will be able to watch the sun setting and the emerging of stars on the dark night sky, This is a beautiful feeling you will not get anywhere, but in Fiji. The service of this restaurant is very good too. All along you will enjoy your stay here in the Emaho Sekawa Resort.

9. Tokoriki Island Resort

Located on the Mamanuca Islands, this resort is restricted only to adults; this resort has some of the best activities to offer to its guests. All of these will keep you engaged here all along with the beautiful surroundings. The lavish rooms and the gorgeous outdoor will make your stay a wonderful experience.

Summarizing: While travelling in a different country it is very important where you are staying, the hotel or the resort will make half of your holiday. So choose wisely where you stay. Fiji is a beautiful country and it offers some of the best places and resorts to stay so you might not need to get all confused and can just pick according to your taste.

Chapter 10: Local Dishes You Must Try in Fiji

Picture Courtesy: Epicure & Culture

Fijian food carries a great deal of culture and tradition with it. They have some of the best traditional food and are very proud to present them in front of the world. From local dishes to seasonal dishes they are very much aware of their preparations and try to make it as healthy as possible. Some of the Fijian food has a regional variety of Indian and Japanese food which is very popular among the locals and the visitors.

1. Rourou

Rourou is just like spinach, it's the Dalo or Taro leaves. The preparations are also like spinach and can be served in various ways. But the best traditional Fijian dish involves the cooking of rourou leaves in an underground earth oven, which is known as Lovo. Another preparation that is very famous in Fiji is the Fijian Rourou Peti. Here the rourou is stuffed with a mixture of chili onion, coconut milk and tune fish. This green dish can be had with bread and as a side dish. This dish is truly a Fijian dish that you should try in Fiji.

2. Coconut Bread

This bread is one of the best food you need to try in Fiji. It is a signature dish in Fiji. In Fiji the coconut is known as the tree of life, and it is involved in many ways in the life of the people of Fiji. Many of the recipes include this coconut and the main ingredient. The coconut bread has been in the Fiji for hundreds of years now and one of the most delicious food staples in this culture. You can have coconut bread with almost everything. Any dish can be complimented with this signature styled bread. And many of the restaurants will serve you only this bread.

3. Lamb Stew

This is one of the finest Fijian foods. The famous lamb stew is a must-try dish in Fiji. This is a traditional food and you will see it in every menu in every restaurant. This traditional food is a part of every event and occasion in Fiji. Here the lamb is cooked with potatoes and carrots and seasonal vegetables. The lamb is cooked until it is falling off the bones. This soft and fantastic dish is best savored with coconut bread and you will fall in love with this Fijian dish.

4. Nama

Nama, also known as green caviar is basically the name of the sea grapes in Fiji. Here they are harvested and grown in shallow waters. These special kind of grapes have some special healing powers and contain lots of goodness and Vitamin A and C. This food is a great substitute for fish and eggs. It can be also savored as a vegan dish, this nama can be cooked into various preparations as well.

5. Lolo Buns

Lolo buns are the Fijian coconut buns that tastes and looks as good and sophisticated as it can be. These buns are often served at breakfast with ice tea or hot coffee. This semi sweet dish is a great dish to start your day with great fun. These bread buns are first soaked in coconut milk then fried until they are golden brown. You will just love this dish specially made in Fiji.

6. Kokoda

Kokoda is the national dish of Fiji and one of the must-try dishes. Kokoda is a dish of fish that is marinated in citrus juices. .The fish can be anything from mahi mahi to any fresh local fish. In fact in restaurants you can choose your own fish. After the fish are caught, they are fixed with coconut cream, onions, chilis and tomatoes. Full of spices this dish is served in a festive way. This dish is very popular among the tourists as it has that unique taste that you might not get anywhere in the world other than Fiji.

7. Cassava Cake

Cassava cake is just like rice cakes. With that same sticky rice that are topped with your favorite toppings from sweet to salty. This rice cakes are known as Cassava in Fiji but Tapioca and Sago in other regions. These cassava cakes are very delicious and can be topped with butter, fresh fruits or whatever you prefer. You might find this dish differently presented in different restaurants with different tastes.

8. Custard Pie

This is a very famous Fijian dessert you cannot miss. This delicious dish is made with cookies and looks like a cake. The creamy and smooth custard will melt in your mouth with just one bite. This dish is very popular among the people of Fiji and many restaurants serve this dish in various ways. It is also a staple food in Fiji. It is a kind of potato or baked bread.

9. Palusami

This dish is made of rourou or taro leaves. Here the leaves are first stuffed with meat or beef and that is mixed with coconut. Mainly this dish has the stuffing of various kinds of meat abut sea food is included in some of the menus. But mostly this dish includes corned beef and it has been a traditional one as for the availability of corn beef at that time when fresh meat was not much available on the island. Palusami is one of the traditional dishes in Fiji and worth tasting it.

10. Fish Soup

As being an island Fiji has plenty of seafood available in the markets. And you can get just the fresh one here. Vacationing on a famous island and not tasting a great seafood dish is not a good thing. The fish soup is said to be the best seafood dish in Fiji. Though the ingredients may vary from region to region, but overall it is the same soup you will find in the restaurants. Maximum of this dish is made with coconut milk. This dish has a special taste of tanginess in it with an addition of lemon and ginger. This dish is very easy to make and can be a great food for lunch and dinner.

Summarizing: Fijian food can be a great delight. They serve the most comfort food with so subtle taste that you will just fall in love with the food. They are not heavy and is totally great for your health. From veg to non-veg you can get every item here in Fijian dishes. The desserts are as much tasty as the seafood of here, packed with nutrition all of the dishes are a must-try in Fiji.

Chapter 11: Things to Avoid in Fiji

Pictures Courtesy: <u>World Nomads</u>

Like all other countries, Fiji has some laws and rules that everyone have to follow. From behaving to dressing, they have some disciple that they maintain. So it is up to the tourists that they have to go by the rules.

1. *Don't Be Afraid when You See a Man Walking With Machetes*

It is pretty obvious for people walking with machetes with them; actually it is very common in Fiji. They prefer this thing while going out for a walk. They just use this to cut grass or break a coconut. Just don't get scared when you locate someone with this dangerous tool as it is very normal for them. And you have nothing to worry. In fact you might see some of the old ladies carry these machetes as well with them in the rural areas.

2. Don't Walk at Night

Fiji is definitely one of the safest places you will visit. But it requires some common sense in that it is a strange and unknown place you should not stay out late at night. If not for the question of safety, it can be due to various reasons. For women travelers, who are travelling solo or with their girlfriends, try to avoid the late night parties. If needed ask your hotel for a taxi. It is better to avail some vehicle rather than walking. It can also be applied to the male travelers as well.

3. Don't Escape from the Words Bula and Vinaka

English is definitely the official language in Fiji, but there are two words that you will be hearing a lot in Fiji. Fijians are very good with their English, but they cannot resist these two words. The two words, Bula and Vinaka mean 'greetings' and 'thank you' respectively. It is just like the word aloha in Hawaii. And it is kind of great to pronounce the words as well. It will let you feel the tradition from a very close angle. So you do not need to learn all the words in Fiji but atleast learn these two words. The Fijians will also love to hear their guests saying these words.

4. Don't Cross the Speed Limit of 80kmh

Like other laws in other country. Fiji has some laws that all have to follow. The speed limit in Fiji is enforced by the police and you might need to pay a fine once caught. So better watch out your speed while driving. Driving around Fiji can be very overwhelming. It is one of the best things you can do in Fiji. The traffic of Fiji can get very fussy, so to avoid this try not to overtake other cars. One minor crash can lead up to great pandemonium right in the middle of the street.

5. Don't Take the Mosquitoes Easily

Mosquitoes can be a very common threat to the people vacationing in Fiji. This island is famous for its mosquitoes. So no matter where you go or what you enjoy, try to keep a mosquito repellent with you and apply it every time you think you are under attack, especially during the evening and the night. In fact Fiji is listed as one of the countries with the infamous Zika virus. This can be a great threat to your health. Watch out for this, so that your fun times in Fiji do not turn into sick times.

6. Don't Go for a Village Tour

Fiji has some of the best beaches. And the resorts of this place are best for your stay. But at some point it might bring you boredom. So instead of staying at resorts it can be a very good idea to visit the villages nearby. Many tourists don't give much attention to the villages. But they are one of the best places you can visit in Fiji. If you want to experience the true Fijian culture and tradition, you must go to the villages. The village tours can be mesmerizing. Here you will find a different way of life full of natural aura and the traditional touch. In fact at the end of the tour you will be greeted with their special handcrafted souvenirs.

7. Don't Get Scared Seeing an Animal

Fiji is very much of an animal friendly country. From stray dogs to cows, you will see them everywhere in the country. If lucky you might get to see horses too. They can be just in the middle of the road barking or mooing or having their food. It is quite normal here and the locals are accustomed to this. So watch out for them. And if you see any, do not get sacred. It is normal out here.

8. Don't Buy Anything Imported

Some food in Fiji can be very expensive. If is the imported one then there are chances that it will be very expensive. So it is better to avoid them and opt for the local food. The local fruits and vegetables are the best food you can have in here. They are very cheap and fresh. You will see the price difference of the same product if you are buying it from a supermarket, you will get it for 5$ while in the local markets they are very cheap, probably a dollar or two. Apart from the food, try to buy all your souvenirs from the local market as you might get it at a lower price.

9. Don't Plan Your Day on Sunday

All the Sundays of Fiji are unofficial a holiday for the people of Fiji. Sundays are basically church day. So all the people are in church dressed in traditional dresses. Many shops and other establishments remain closed on Sundays. Or if open, they might be so for limited hours. So it is better to have all of your shopping done before Sunday. Apart from this, as Fiji has a big Fijian-Indian Population, here you might see some of the festivals related to Hinduism.

10. Don't Wear Your Two Pieces Everywhere

While on a beach, especially like the beaches in Fiji, a two piece or swimming dress can be very flattering. But as much as the people of Fiji like them, there are many places which have a more conservative dress code, especially in those small villages. So wear your dresses accord9ngly. Women should always cover their shoulder, not only women, men also have to follow some of the rules, when it comes to dressing.

Summarizing: As a new country all the visitors are obliged to maintain the laws and go by them. Fiji has a very cultural aspect so when it comes to their life style and living, they are very much bounded with their tradition and culture. So they have to follow some rules to maintain discipline. And so is expected from all the tourists to do the same as well.

Chapter 12: Conclusion

Picture Courtesy: <u>Hilton</u>

The tourism industry of Fiji is getting enormous day by day. The biggest source of tourists being the countries like Australia, USA , New Zealand and more. The significant amount of the natural resources and natural wonders has made Fiji one of the great travel destinations in the world. The popular regions like Nadi, Denarau Island and the Mamanuca Isalnds have become the main tourist attractions. The soft coral reefs, the great spots for scuba diving, and those perfect settings of white sandy beaches, that great tropical climate and the aesthetically pleasing islands with best holiday destinations, all are here. With the special spa treatment with their very own natural sources, the world class five star resorts have provided a treatment of luxury to the every guest of Fiji. In Fiji you will get everything for relaxation and solitude that you have been seeking for all this time. This country has an aura that will make all your worries melt down. This country will give you the opportunity to see nature very closely. You can also get lost into the lap of mysterious places and secret waterfalls; the exploration of this paces is surly a bliss for the travelers and explorers. The uniqueness of Fiji and its culture makes it as one of the top island destinations for the tourists. This land of many lands is surely a place to visit at least once in a life time.

Made in the USA
Coppell, TX
25 March 2023